TWELFTH CENTURY PAINTINGS

AT

HARDHAM & CLAYTON

INTRODUCTORY ESSAY

by

CLIVE BELL

PHOTOGRAPHS BY HELMUT GERNSHEIM

PUBLISHED AND EDITED BY
FRANCES BYNG-STAMPER & CAROLINE LUCAS

MILLER'S PRESS
LEWES, SUSSEX
1947

ACKNOWLEDGEMENT

Without the scholarship, enthusiasm and good humour of Dr. F. Saxl this book could not have been produced.

Iconographical Notes by Dr. Robert Freyhan

Tracings by Caroline Lucas

Elevations by Frances Allen

Printed at the Chiswick Press, London

CONTENTS

INTRODUCTORY ESSAY

HERE ARE forty remarkable photographs: extraordinary one might call them. They are out of the ordinary because they are genuine reproductions of twelfth-century paintings. What we are shown is what actually exists on the walls of two Sussex churches—Clayton and Hardham. Also, these untitivated photographs are beautiful; they contrive to be honest without being poor. That they are fragmentary goes without saying. The paintings are in what, were we considering work of three or four hundred years later, we should call "shocking condition". They are broken and blurred and as often as not illegible almost: even so are the photographs. These show us no more than the most powerful and intelligently manipulated lens can see; which is rather more than the naked eye can see. That is all. If aesthetically and iconographically Mr. Gernsheim's reproductions seem incomplete that is for the very good reason that the originals are incomplete.

Inevitably, perhaps unfortunately, these photographs challenge comparison with the plates published last year by Professor Tristram in his *English Medieval Wall Painting: The Twelfth Century*; for in that volume the paintings at Clayton and Hardham were handsomely presented and discussed. As I shall soon be criticising let me at once salute this stately production, a monument of industry; and let me add that the extent of my debt to it will be appreciated by anyone who does me the honour of reading this essay. Unluckily, the illustrations are not reproductions of twelfth-century paintings but of water-colour drawings by the author. These may have iconographical value, though that would be greater had the water-colourist refrained from supplementing what is visible by what he thinks should be: aesthetically, they are, in my opinion, worthless. Frankly, they are not like the originals. Let critics put this assertion to the test by comparing the professor's sketches with Mr. Gernsheim's records; or, better still, by coming into Sussex and seeing for themselves. If it be contended, by way of excuse, that the paintings are so placed as to make photographing them impossible, here are exhibits to prove the contrary. Moreover, M. Pierre Devinoy had already before the war taken and published successful photographs of twelfth-century paintings every bit as awkwardly situated as those of which Professor Tristram has been content to make sketches. What is still more, he had given an account of how he took them. I must add that this collection, *Peintures Romanes* (*Hartmann, Paris* 1938), enriched with a learned essay by Prof. Henri Focillon, is one that every student should keep by him. Indeed the serious student of English twelfth-century painting will be constantly in debt to French scholarship, and, if ever again it becomes possible, should make frequent visits to France. For it would seem that France in the twelfth century produced painting as copiously almost as in the nineteenth: also, the quality is generally high, and, what is not unimportant to students, much, though by no means all, has been adequately photographed. In England we have far less, and of what we have a good deal is second- or third-rate. But one advantage we do enjoy: our paintings have rarely been improved. French twelfth-century painting, discovered a hundred years ago by Merimée, was taken in hand, first by his friend Viollet-le-duc, then by Viollet-le-duc's disciples and successors, with what results can be imagined.[1]

[1] In 1900 the paintings at Hardham were cleaned and varnished; whether for better or for worse is matter of opinion.

The fine and faithful photographs about which I have been asked to say a word are of paintings at Clayton (about ten miles from Lewes) and at Hardham (about a mile from Pulborough). Hardham is thought to have been decorated in 1125 and Clayton perhaps twenty-five years later.[1] But to win from these none too yielding works all the pleasure they have to give it is necessary, I fear, to know something of what had been going on in France and England during the preceding century. In the eleventh was opening that lovely flower which came to blossom in the twelfth: we call it Romanesque. The twelfth century is, I suppose, the most brilliant in West European history between the death of Virgil and the birth of Petrarch. Splendid in painting, sculpture, architecture, glass; promising in poetry; acute in thought; it was an age of art and an age of heresies. How it came to being, and why it died untimely, are questions without our purview. Only these facts should be borne in mind: with the establishment in the later ninth century of the Macedonian dynasty a second golden age dawned at Byzantium; the splendour endured under the Comneni almost to the end of the twelfth; in 1096 the first crusaders reached Constantinople. Not to connect Romanesque art with these events seems to me impossible.

West of Byzantine territories, in the late tenth and the eleventh century, the Anglo-Saxon school of drawing, with its centre at Winchester, was doubtless the most accomplished. The elegance, liveliness and precision of these miniatures, when one comes on reproductions of them, as one often does—for the frontispiece to King Edgar's charter and pages from the Chatsworth Benedictional are freely reproduced—positively take one's breath away. "What skill!", we exclaim, "What science! These penmen had little to learn from anybody." Yet it has been said that with the Norman Conquest the English tradition vanished. I do not believe it. Not so quickly is a great tradition smothered. Why, at Hardham there may have been men working whose fathers had worked for the Confessor: to be sure, the Hardham man was a wall-painter and the man who worked for King Edward probably an illustrator, and therefore probably a monk, so let us say "uncle".[2] Anyhow, it is a mistake to suppose that Anglo-Saxon art in the eleventh century was a nook-shotten affair of purely local import, easily rooted out. Was it not the Englishman, Courland, who built St. Hilaire-le-grand at Poitiers, one of the eminent achievements of the age? So very much alive appears Anglo-Saxon art in the eleventh century, so vigorous and accomplished is the work of the Winchester school, that at times one is tempted to regret the disruptive activities of those Norman roughs.[3] It is a temptation to be resisted. The Conqueror finished the work that the Confessor had barely begun, finished it brutally but efficiently. He bridged the channel, and put England firmly and for good in touch with France and the continent beyond. Doubtless the Norman conquest was one of those blessings that are only too apt to come in disguise.

[1] These dates have been disputed.

[2] As a matter of fact, the English school was remarkably secular in its tastes, preferring to illustrate Psalters and Calendars—in which liberties could be taken and into which bits of mundane realism could be introduced—rather than to illuminate devoutly Liturgical books.

[3] The Normans, those greatly gifted architects, had little talent for painting and drawing.

The twelfth is pre-eminently a French century; but that does not mean that Anglo-Saxon influence disappeared as suddenly as the swallows. Only the other day at Canterbury, where, thanks to the amiability of Canon Potts, the powerful lamp of a photographer and a pile of packing-cases, I was able to see the paintings in St. Gabriel's chapel as I had never seen them before, one of the things that struck me was the distinct trace of a persistent English tradition. I noticed the fluttering play of drapery, in which the Anglo-Saxons, with their lively and commanding pens, delighted, whereas the French masters of the perfect Romanesque style, influenced some think by the nude figures of classical sculpture, tend to treat drapery almost as though it were an outer skin. I admired in St. Anselm's the fluent, unhesitating line that describes the contour of the bending apostle, and again I noticed the nice rapidity with which the folds of drapery are indicated and the certainty with which the movement of limbs is defined. This took me back to Winchester of the preceding century. And it is to be remembered that Canterbury and Lewes— it is to the Lewes school, of course, that our paintings belong—were not the only twelfth-century schools in the country, and that Lewes, as we shall see, was of all the most French. There were schools at Winchester, Norwich, Bury St. Edmunds, Durham; and there were others of which too little work remains for us to form any clear idea of their affiliations. But from little of what does remain is the Anglo-Saxon influence completely banished: at least so it seems to me.[1]

French influence was stronger in Sussex than elsewhere. You would expect it to be so. Immediately after the Conquest was founded at Lewes that great Cluniac priory which seemingly became a centre of French civilisation radiating light and, let us hope, some measure of sweetness over this corner of England. As far as the confines of the metropolitan see on the one side and as far as Chichester, as Southampton even, on the other, the influence of Lewes was felt: to the north it seems to have petered out not far short of Guildford. Of the power and glory of this great house let those speak who have the right, first and foremost that fine scholar, Mr. Godfrey, to whom all lovers of Lewes and of beauty owe thanks, and I especial thanks, for generous help and encouragement. Only, in discussing these Sussex paintings I am loth to work Cluny too hard; for, after all, there are no solid grounds for believing that Hardham was a Cluniac church, though Clayton certainly was, while those churches in central and south-western France (e.g. St. Savin, Liget), to whose paintings the learned, rightly no doubt, relate ours, were by no means all Clunisien.[2] Whether the church at Vic was dependent on Cluny I do not know, but it is not cited in Miss Evans's authoritative work[3]: yet it is with the paintings in this church that ours are most often compared. These Vic paintings, by the way, are to French scholars a puzzle. "D'où vient cet art?"

[1] Of an entirely unsupported hypothesis of my own—a notion that some of the daintiness and drama of the thirteenth-century may have been, as it were, a throw-back to the Anglo-Saxon tradition, I say nothing. Or, only this: have another look at the paintings in the chapel of the Holy Sepulchre at Winchester and in the Bishop's private chapel at Chichester.

[2] Not till the fifteenth century did the Prior of Lewes become patron of the Hardham living: at least not till 1430 is there any record of a presentation by the Cluniac house.

[3] Romanesque architecture of the order of Cluny (Cambridge).

exclaims Focillon, "*Quelle est sa source?*" "*Par la technique, nous le jugeons plus près de l'art de l'Ouest que de la manière clunisienne. Mais dans la France romane à laquelle il appartient pourtant, il nous faut bien reconnaître que, jusqu' à present, aucun mur d'église ne nous a montré un style semblable, ou seulement analogue.*" God forbid I should suggest that "cet art" came from Sussex. It is bad enough one should be bound to admit that Constable influenced French painting in the nineteenth century without having to suppose that another English painter carried weight in the twelfth. But I will venture a startling hypothesis: maybe all these artists, the master of Vic and the masters of Clayton and Hardham, painted in the way they did because they felt that way. Such things have happened before and since.[1]

This explanation, I am aware, will not suit the book, or books, of those experts for whom every figure and gesture, every line and blot, must be sponsored by something that went before. Everything in a work of art, they hold, must come from somewhere else; and probably they will explain the paintings at Vic by a prototype of which all trace has been lost. This question of prototypes is so important to the student of twelfth-century painting and sculpture that, at the risk of becoming a bore, I will say a word about it. Far be it from me to re-hash the shrewd arguments of Diehl and Strzygowski, about which I once knew a good deal more than I can remember: besides, Prof. Emile Mâle, to whose ingenious work, *L'Art religieux du XIIme siècle* I refer the reader, has made the matter much simpler. Very roughly the theory is this. Before the days of Justinian, that is to say before the formation of a Byzantine style, sacred books were being written, illustrated and copied; and the copying was done by monks, most of whom were not artists, many of whom, therefore, reproduced the illustrations as scrupulously and as unintelligently as they reproduced the text. If ever men deserved the name of "sedulous apes" it was they. Yet even then there was diversity: the very monks made innovations. Moreover, there were two distinct schools of illustrators and copyists: for whereas the Hellenistic monks worked in what was left of a classical and realistic tradition, the monks of Syria and Asia Minor worked in the oriental, and were consequently more abstract, decorative and senti-mental. Most of the originals, the veritable prototypes, are supposed to have perished; but monks being monks, that is "sedulous apes"—such is the theory —all the illustrated manuscripts of the dark and early middle ages are supposed to be more or less faithful copies of what was done in the fourth and fifth centuries. Wherefore, say the pundits, all existing medieval miniatures can be grouped in families and traced to a common, if unknown, ancestor; and to these miniatures, and therefore indirectly to their ancestors, Roman-esque painters, sculptors, glass-makers, carvers, goldsmiths, textile-designers and workers in enamel had all to go for their facts. They had to get their subjects right by the book, right historically, right theologically and right liturgically. I do not doubt it. What I do venture to doubt is whether they

[1] This hypothesis may come in useful to anyone who has to account for the extra-ordinary paintings at Tavant (Indre et Loire), which, since it seems unlikely that they were influenced by certain eighth-century paintings in the crypt of S. Clemente in Rome or by early Matisse—the only works with which they can well be com-pared—provide archaeologists with another stumbling-block.

vent to the books for their art. Subject and treatment are two things. The
tatement will strike you as obvious; but it may come as a surprise to certain
rchaeologists.[1]

To return to Cluny. It is certain that the parent house had immense and
beneficial influence on the whole Burgundian region, and that the Cluniac
establishment at La Charité was hardly less serviceable to central and south-
western France, nor need we doubt that the Priory of St. Pancras at Lewes
played a like part on a smaller stage. Whether one should say more than that
—which after all is a good deal—I hardly know. However, science has come
o the aid of those who see the finger of Cluny in all the best pies, in the
eminent person of M. Fernand Mercier.[2] This savant distinguishes confidently
between "La peinture clunysienne" which he designates "brillante" and
'la peinture romane", which he considers "mate." He has analyzed chemi-
cally the paintings—and lovely paintings they are—in the little church of
Berzé-la-ville, a Cluniac chapel not far from the parent house, and has
discovered an elaborate system of under-paintings and glazes very different,
n his opinion, from the comparatively straightforward wash-work which he
considers the proper Romanesque technique. Who dares gainsay the dictates
of Science? All the same, I will venture to suggest that a point of logic remains.
Granting the distinction of techniques, do we know for certain that all paint-
ngs in the brilliant manner and no paintings in the other are Clunysien?
M. Mercier has not yet analysed all the paintings in all the churches, and when
he has it will remain for someone else to decide precisely which churches
depended on Cluny. When next you take your walks abroad—supposing you
are ever permitted to do such a thing—I shall not be surprised if you find
examples of "brillante" painting in admittedly uncluniacal places and
'mate" in churches dependent on the Abbey. Meanwhile, may I advise
archaeologists not to rely entirely on criteria supplied by chemistry, for this
very scientific reason—they cannot control them.[3]

Microchemistry and radiochemistry, to say nothing of spectrography, are
all very well, I am sure, and may prove anything in time, but I doubt whether
they can supply unexceptionable attributions and affiliations yet. Chemical
criticism is in its infancy, and neither the archaeologists nor I know enough
about it to check the results. My notion is that peculiarities and differences of
technique in the twelfth century are likely to have been caused by geography
and economics as much as by doctrine and discipline, that the influences be-

[1] Prof. Mâle, who, for all that he seems to consider Claus Sluter of Dijon a match for Michelangelo, has a feeling for art, admits that artists will be artists, i.e., creators and inventors. And, talking of prototypes, may I, in my ignorance, be allowed to wonder how a twelfth-century artist, commissioned to re-count the adventures of some obscure local saint or hero of romance, could have found illustrated books to guide him?

[2] La peinture clunysienne. Fernand Mercier.

[3] Nevertheless, had Prof. Tristram con-rasted the paintings of Clayton and Hard-man with those at Berzé-la-ville, the comparison might have yielded useful results. The painting at Hardham has, I understand, been analysed by the Courtauld Institute. As anyone can see for himself, at both Clayton and Hardham the flesh tints were under-painted with "veneda" (black). But this will not much help the argument, seeing that such underpainting is recommended by the monk Theophilus and was employed in Cluniac and non-Cluniac churches through-out northern Europe.

hind the Lewes style are as much regional as religious. Artists would hav
adapted to their purposes the material they found to hand; and what the
found to hand in Sussex and Surrey, poor and outlandish places, were th
cheap earth colours. Of the rare and expensive—blue, green, vermilion—yo
will not see much. Yet both green and vermilion were used at Hardham
from which I infer that an artist of force and reputation generally got his way
employed the technique that seemed to him appropriate and procured some
how the colours he needed.

He who is not overawed by the wonders of science will hardly be put dow
by stylistic demonstrations. Attentive readers will have observed that I am
myself, a stylistic critic: may they also have observed that I am one who con
ceives it possible he may mistake. Of stylistic criticism, applied to modern o
comparatively modern work, operating therefore in cases where abundan
evidence of other kinds is obtainable, I have had some experience, and know
into what troubles it can drag an unwary adept. That a Cluniac style existed
seems as certain as that a Barbizon style existed: but when we have to deter
mine, on stylistic grounds, whether a particular picture was painted in
particular place at a precise date under the influence of a known master or
definite school we are far from the world of certainties. It is one thing to say—
a Cluniac style existed, and quite another to say this figure or fragment i
Clunisien. So, if neither chemical nor stylistic evidence is to be reckoned
quite conclusive, entitling us to say dogmatically—these Sussex painting
are Clunisien, we must fall back on iconography.

For iconographical evidence I had always felt the respect proper to ignor
ance. One morning, however, clambering about the scaffolding at Hardham
I heard, or thought I heard, the immensely learned and hardly less witty
director of the Warburg Institute let fall a comment which led me to surmise
that he did not consider the findings of iconologists infallible. I may have
misinterpreted a passing jest; but ever since I have seemed to catch in the
conversation of the wise and witty a faint note of scepticism. And, to be sure
in a battered, peeled, chipped, discoloured wall-painting it is possible to mis
take a bishop for a donkey or a stain for a beast of the Apocalypse. Also, from
personal experience, I must confess that, once a particular mass has been
identified with an historical or mythological person or event it is surprisingly
easy to make other masses assume characters which fit into the scene which
one imagines to be depicted. I speak only for myself, of course, for mysel
and for the apprentices of the trade. It is not to be supposed that masters,
such as Mâle and Panofsky, make such blunders. No one, I dare say, ha
known more about early Christian iconology than Emile Mâle, and few have
spoken with more confidence on that or any other subject. Here is his
considered opinion: *"L'iconographie du XIIme siècle est pleine de bizarreries,
d'incohérences et de contradictions."* It behoves amateurs, then, to be cautious.
Unprompted, the only indisputable bit of Clunyism I was able to discover at
Clayton, albeit a Cluniac church, was the prominence given to St. Peter
receiving the keys and St. Paul receiving the book. Peter and Paul were prime
favourites at Cluny. On the other hand, the prominence given to the
Torments of the Damned at Clayton and Hardham and perhaps at Witley,
has been learnedly ascribed to the influence of St. Denis, which was building

and decorating in the first half of the twelfth century: Suger, as even I knew, having a peculiar taste for the subject.

The influence of St. Denis on the Sussex school is duly noted by Professor Tristram, who goes so far as to say that "the twelfth-century revival in this country synchronised with that on the Continent, when the Abbey of St. Denis, under Abbot Suger, *became the centre of the new movement, on the fringe of which England stood*" (my italics). Sussex, then, is an outpost of Denisien or Dionysien culture. A little later, in more positive mood, the Professor tells us that "a number of paintings in Surrey and Sussex" (Clayton and Hardham amongst them) "all with clearly defined and marked characteristics, may be regarded as emanating from one source. The evidence to support the theory that they are all of Cluniac workmanship, and inspired by the Priory of St. Pancras at Lewes, the chief Cluniac house in this country, is sufficiently strong to place the matter beyond doubt." That's that. The one difficulty remaining is that St. Denis was not a Cluniac house. Assuredly Suger employed artists and artisans from Cluny—amongst other places. He employed the best to be had from no matter where. He summoned them to Paris from all over France, from Lorraine, from the Midi, from all over Europe maybe. The art of St. Denis was national, not to say cosmopolitan: it was not Clunysien. We shall find it easier to believe Professor Tristram when he has told us what to believe. Are these Sussex paintings Clunysien or Sugeresque?

If you are bent—which I am not—on finding one predominant influence, I should have thought it would be prudent to take refuge in that blessed word "Byzantine". Byzantine influence in the twelfth century, it seems to me, was pretty much what French influence was in the nineteenth and early twentieth: it was inescapable. That grand, hieratic ordering of the composition which is the very hall-mark of Romanesque, distinguishing it sharply from the prettier and more dramatic Gothic; that inflexible habit of regarding the picture-space as two-dimensional; that resolute closing of the hole in the wall: are not these Byzantine legacies? To descend to details: the intense gaze of wide-open eyes is probably a reference, direct or indirect, to the technique of the mosaicists, as are the absence of gradations and the juxtaposition of pure tones to produce an effect of solidity. To sink lower and come still nearer home: in certain angelic figures at both Clayton and Hardham is to be seen a curious crossing of the arms which, I am given to understand, is a Greek gesture signifying intercession. While, believe it or not, at Hardham and at West-meston the Lamb of God faces left. This is most irregular. In orthodox Christendom, however, it would be quite in order, seeing that, in those parts, so the scholars tell us, the left is the side of honour. Need I say that for these startling bits of erudition I am in debt to the Professor? All things considered, I incline to the theory that, behind secondary influences, French, Anglo-Saxon, Cluniac, Dionysien, stands the pervasive power and prestige of the Eastern empire and ensample of the Macedonian masters.

Having adumbrated, imperfectly and with unbecoming levity perhaps, the findings of the experts, may I now give my appreciation of these paintings and my notion of how they were done? That I shall be snubbed for my pains by some recognized authority goes without saying; but I take comfort in the thought that my corrector himself will probably be treated not much better by some authority not less eminent. In the first place, then, let us get it out of our heads that medieval wall-painters were necessarily monks. There is no reason to believe that secular artists were not as numerous as cloistered: the romantic picture of churches built and decorated throughout by consecrated hands is proven bosh. Nor is the notion of a community, a congeries of common men, rushing Gadarenewise into creation and raising a perfect work of art, more commendable. These paintings were made by individual artists, assisted by pupils no doubt. As a matter of fact, Romanesque artists were not all anonymous, nor were all Carolingian if it comes to that, though I doubt whether anyone knows the name of a man who painted a particular wall. Be that as it may, no great work ever came into being but conceived and dared by a single mind; though it may have been executed by a multitude of hands, and in the case of architecture must have been.

The twelfth-century painter commissioned to decorate a church would presumably have been given a book in which were depicted in miniature the scenes he was to display at large. This book would be his guide and source of reference: hence the importance of miniatures to students of iconography in wall-painting. A timid, unimaginative decorator would follow his book scrupulously: a bold, original artist would do no such thing. He would draw or scratch on the plaster a scheme of what he meant to do; and, unless I mistake, there exists in the crypt at Canterbury a fragment of wall or pillar which has been so scratched and still bears the outline of a project which for one reason or another was never carried out. Also, beneath the paint in medieval churches sometimes we find the roughly indicated idea and can see for ourselves how far the artist has departed from it.[1] Having made his sketch, our artist—our bold, original artist—would wait till it had been given what his descendants call the O.K., what he may have called the S.F. (*satis fecit*), by some doctor who could pronounce the project theologically, historically and liturgically correct, who could guarantee the propriety of the attributes, make sure the emblems were appropriate and generally arm the painter against ecclesiastical objections. This granted, the artist, I imagine, followed his bent, paying no excessive attention to his own scribblings, his guide-book or the advice tendered by passing divines. We know that he did not always stick to his text, and that sometimes he changed his mind; for we find *pentimenti*, departures from the original plan, and diversity of treatment inconceivable in a miniature. I do not suggest that painters did exactly as they pleased. I do surmise that they took liberties and were expected to take them. Did not that formidable canonist, Guillaume Durand, quote with approval the Horatian licence—

"*Diversae historiae tam Novi quam Veteris Testamenti pro voluntate pictorum depinguntur: nam*

    '. . . . . . . *pictoribus atque poetis*
     Quidlibet audendi semper fuit aequa potestas.'"

It was from the floor that I first saw the paintings at Hardham and

---

[1] Mr Wittemore has shown that the masters who set the mosaics in Sta. Sophia adopted similar methods.

Clayton, and I came to the conclusion that the former were the better. When the scaffolding had been put up to accommodate Mr. Gernsheim and his camera I had opportunities of considering the work more closely; and then I changed my mind. I could see that the Clayton frescoes—for frescoes they will be called by all but sticklers for minute technical distinctions—were highly accomplished, masterly in drawing, and conceived intelligently as a scheme of decoration. By comparison the work at Hardham had a provincial air. Today, with these accurate and revealing photographs to help me, I recognize, or seem to recognize, two distinct styles, and am unwilling to pronounce one superior to the other: also, in both churches I seem to detect the work of more than one hand. This is stylistic criticism with a vengeance: that is why I say "seem". The Clayton paintings, all smeared and battered though they be, seem, then, to be the work of accomplished artists who knew their job—the Romanesque job. The difference between them and the paintings at Hardham is not simply the difference between 1150 and 1125, but perhaps—and this should give pleasure to the Cluniacs—the difference between French-trained and native artists. Observe, however, that my hypothesis, which strengthens the Cluniac argument in the case of Clayton, weakens it in the case of Hardham: indeed, the difference between the two styles appears to me great enough to make hazardous the assigning of the paintings in both churches to one school. If, for convenience, we continue to speak of the "Lewes" or "Sussex" school, let us do so bearing in mind that Renoir and Degas are both described as "Impressionists", which does not imply that their methods or education were much alike.

I do not think the master or masters of Hardham, the home-bred men, could have produced anything so fully realised in the Romanesque manner, so beautifully sure, as the figure giving the Benediction (Plate 26), or the group of mitred heads (Plate 6), or the crowd (Plate 2): the drawing of this last might, without impertinence, be compared with uncooked passages at St. Savin, painted fifty years earlier. Incidentally, the Christ above the chancel arch (Plate 22), a thing of magic, might be compared with certain Byzantine-Sassanian textiles, deeply venerated in France during the dark and early middle ages and esteemed the produce of supernatural beings: but that would be matter for the pen of Emile Mâle. What anyone can see for himself is, that whereas the panels at Clayton, precise and delicate in detail, have yet been conceived in the high Romanesque manner as parts of a decorative whole, at Hardham the conception is primarily descriptive. The Hardham men are still preoccupied, not to say perplexed, by the difficulty of telling a long story. The masters of Clayton have solved these elementary problems, and can devote their powers to creating an aesthetically satisfying unity. In a word, the Clayton paintings are thoroughly in the Romanesque, that is, the French movement. Not that they lack character of their own; for instance, I know of nothing in France quite like the bold and expressive drawing of hands and arms in Judgment Day (Plate 12), unless it be certain flying limbs by that reckless and original master of Tavant. But let me say honestly, and with due humility, that in these Clayton paintings I find little trace of Anglo-Saxon influence.

At Hardham, on the other hand, the most striking panel, The Temptation

(Plate 29), just within the chancel, is apparently related to some English miniature. This work, one can scarcely doubt, is by an artist who took no hand in the rest of the decoration. It is a thing apart, luckily in excellent condition, of which the elegance is easily appreciated; and no critic is needed to point out that essentially it is a drawing, the quality of which depends on line at once fluent and nervous. For the rest, we must enjoy these Hardham paintings as separate panels rather than as continuous design. And enjoyable they are—enjoyable and something more. Such compositions as The Baptism (Plate 37) and Virgin and Child (Plate 32), albeit worn and largely obliterated, are of a monumental grandeur and profoundly moving. I doubt whether there is anything at Clayton so deeply felt and by sheer rightness of relations so impressive. The Chinese effect of the figures on the south-east wall of the Choir (Plate 28) is presumably accidental, the result of wear and tear: or will some greatly daring Sinologue come forward with a theory of extreme-oriental influence infiltrating through Turkestan and Bagdad? Anyhow, there is nothing fortuitous about the pencilling which has been done with Anglo-Saxon grace. The figure on a horse apparently spearing a beast—(Plate 33)—some take it for a Psychomachia, others for St. George—may well have been re-touched by Gothic hands, and the same comment has been made on the Daemons in Hell (Plate 40). Everyone on entering the church admires the colour. To be sure, it is lovely and mysterious. But I shall not deny that the enchantment of certain passages, the dream-like entanglements, the beautiful merging of tone into tone, may in some measure be due to the dirt and attrition of eight hundred years.

Of characteristics common to both churches—Sussex characteristics we may call them—which I ought to have observed, I shall mention those only that I did observe. We can all see that the walls are divided into tiers and that horizontal bands in red and yellow provide a frame and a background: red and yellow, the cheap colours, predominate. The separating of the panels one from another by strips of architecture is a conspicuous and pleasing custom which adds to the liveliness of the scene. Probably you will observe, since I did, the pretty, long, Italianate letters, more to my taste than the squat characters of Canterbury: for this seemingly we may thank the French. The pigment looks thick and is opaque, and the high lights are intense, all which, let me handsomely admit, are considered Clunisien characteristics. Beneath the flesh-tints is a dark under-painting, and this under-painting as often as not is all the painting that remains. The elongation of the figures, essential to the expressiveness of the design, is said to be another French importation; but here I would put in a word for Byzantium, were it not that elongation and distortion—sometimes called idealization—were commonly and widely employed by artists throughout the dark and middle ages, and have been employed and will be employed wherever and whenever artists worthy the name exist. Nor can the noticeable emphasis on the eyes be reckoned a singularity of the Sussex school, seeing that, besides being a mode of expression used habitually by the mosaicists, it is to be found in many, if not most, of the better productions of the age.

However controversial the points of scholarship they raise, there can be no question that these fragmentary paintings at Clayton and Hardham give a good idea of twelfth-century art, or that Mr. Gernsheim's photographs give a good idea of the paintings. To realise the fundamental difference between Romanesque and Gothic it would, I daresay, suffice to study these. Contrast the monumental grouping of forms, the stately poise of particular figures, the slow, processional movement—hieratic, I would say, thinking always of Byzantium—the impersonal, unromantic attitude of the artist, with what would have been done two hundred years later, and you will feel the difference. Here is nothing melodramatic and little that is agitated even, nothing winsome, nothing sentimental, no figures swinging on the hips or bent on being gracious; but assuredly these Romanesque artists aimed at expression and hit it. They achieved their ends by aesthetic means, like the mosaicists, never hesitating to amplify important forms and significant gestures. They put the accent where it was wanted, not where it fell by chance. If a human being is twice as tall as the house or tree by which he stands that is because the artist felt that the human being was much more important. For the same reason eyes and hands, those emotionally significant members, are magnified out of all natural proportion. This, academic critics in the nineteenth century were incapable of understanding.[1] They seem genuinely to have believed that Romanesque artists tried to paint like the President of the Royal Aacademy, and failed. And when the Impressionists appeared and, at the turn of the century, the Post-Impressionists, these judges made precisely the same mistake. To suppose that the Byzantine masters or the gifted and highly-trained men who decorated Clayton could not have reduced the size of their figures or augmented that of their trees seems to me silly—all the sillier if, like those who judged twelfth-century painters incompetent and childish, you admire hugely twelfth-century architecture. It never struck these critics as odd, one must suppose, that an age which produced master builders should be incapable of producing painters who knew the rudiments of their trade.

The twelfth-century painters had plenty to do. It is just possible that in England the outsides as well as the interiors of churches were decorated, as they still are, or were till quite lately, in the Balkans. This would have been done as much to protect the walls from the weather as to beautify them; and if these works of art bore the brunt of the climate it is not surprising that they perished. Painters were expected also, it seems, to colour statuary and make designs for sculptors. They had their work cut out. And what has become of it all? Some doubtless lies hidden behind coats of whitewash. Much was destroyed by successive generations of painters; for when a new saint or a new style came into fashion the painter made no scruple of obliterating earlier work by superimposing a bed of plaster on which to tell the new story or the old differently. So the artists themselves are the first offenders. Then came Thomas Cromwell and his crew, whose manifold sins are often laid at the door of Oliver—a work of supererogation, for the Protector and his ragamuffins have mischief enough of their own to answer for. We all know of damned Dowsing and his misdoings: he makes boast of them. But the greatest malefactors of all were the nineteenth and perhaps some twentieth-century architects who fancied themselves archaeologists. These wiseacres got it into their heads

[1] Not M. Merimée, however.

that the proper thing to do with a medieval building was to show the scientific construction, to bare the bones as they put it. The notion went, of course, clean contrary to the medieval conception of a church as a vessel of riotous colour and ornament, decorated from roof to floor; but this conception was by no means to the taste of businessmen who wanted to advertise their skill and make money. So they hacked and scraped away whatever traces of colour they could find; and under other rules, in different circumstances, the game goes on. Vandalism, it seems, comes naturally to surveyors and politicians as well as to "the people who love all things beautiful". Nobody is surprised to read in his paper that a work of art has been demolished to make room for a Bank or a Cultural Centre.

CLIVE BELL.

PLATES OF CLAYTON

Plate I ANGEL BLOWING TRUMPET

Plate 2   SOULS AWAITING THEIR FATE

Plate 3   APOCALYPTIC HORSEMAN WITH SOULS AWAITING FATE

Plate 4   APOCALYPTIC HORSEMAN GRASPING THE HEAD OF A MAN

Plate 5 DETAIL OF PLATE 4

Plate 6 CROWNED KINGS (OF THE GROUP OF THE BLESSED)

Plate 7   ANGEL WELCOMING THE BISHOPS (OF THE GROUP OF THE BLESSED)

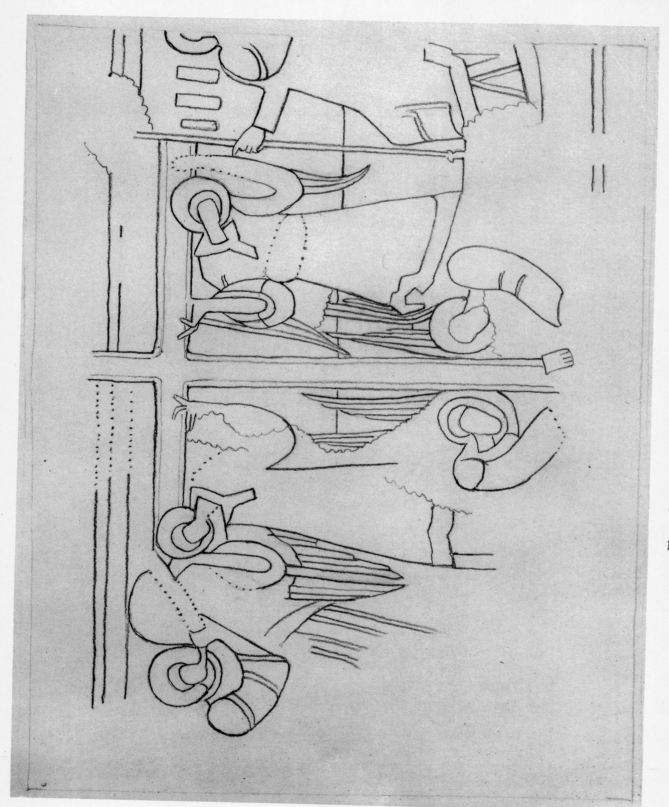

Plate 8 THE CROSS CARRIED BY FOUR ANGELS

Plate 9   DETAILS OF PLATE 8

Plate 10   DEATH OF THE ANTICHRIST (?)

Plate 11   ORDINARY MEN AND FIGURES WEARING CROWNS (OF THE GROUP OF THE BLESSED)

Plate 12   BODIES RISING FROM THE GRAVE

Plate 13   ANGEL HOLDING THE SCALES OF JUSTICE

Plate 14   ANGEL WELCOMING THE BISHOPS

Plate 15   A BISHOP BEING RECEIVED BY A SAINT

Plate 16 DETAIL OF PLATE 15

Plate 17 ENCLOSURE OF THE HEAVENLY JERUSALEM

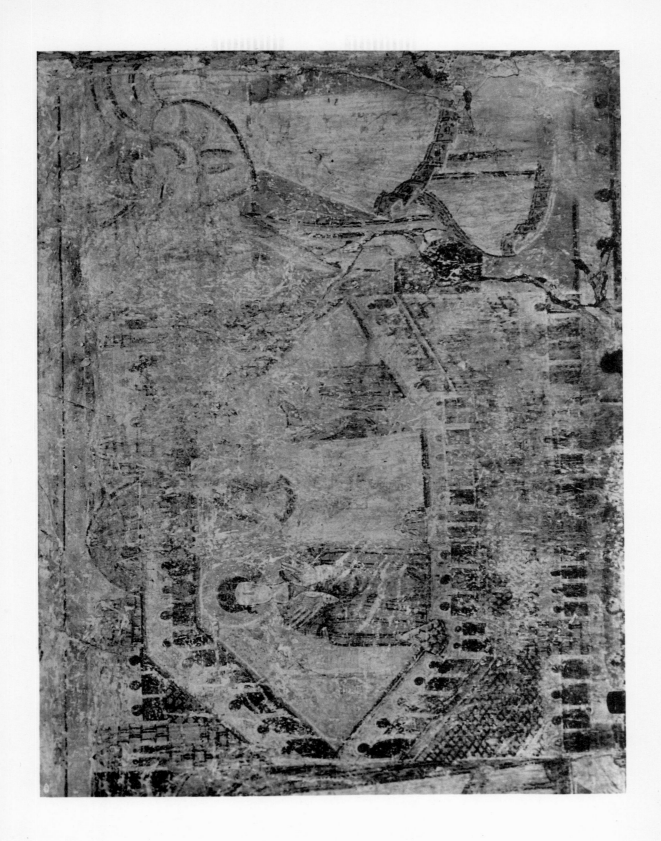

Plate 18   DETAIL OF PLATE 17

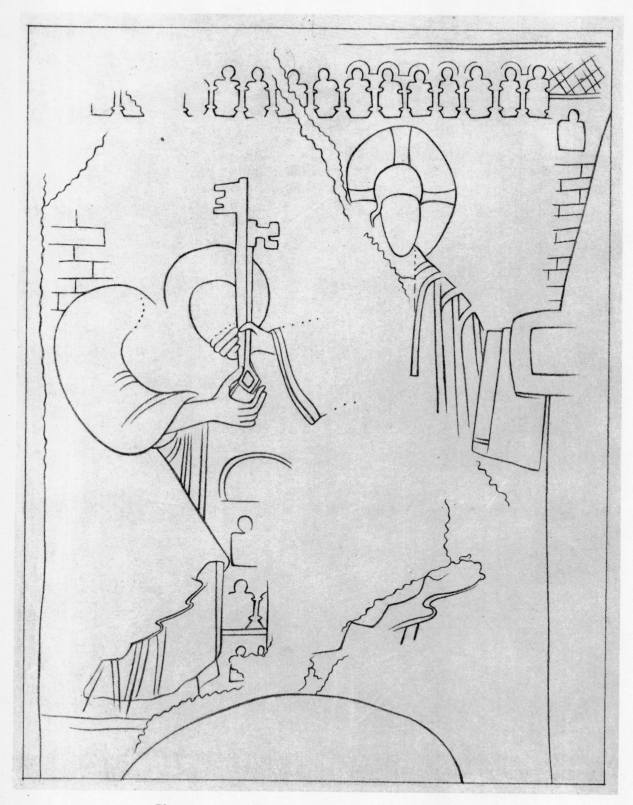

Plate 19   CHRIST DELIVERING THE KEYS TO ST. PETER

Plate 20   APOSTLES ON THE RIGHT OF CHRIST

Plate 21   DETAIL OF PLATE 20

Plate 22   CHRIST IN MAJESTY

Plate 23   APOSTLES ON THE LEFT OF CHRIST

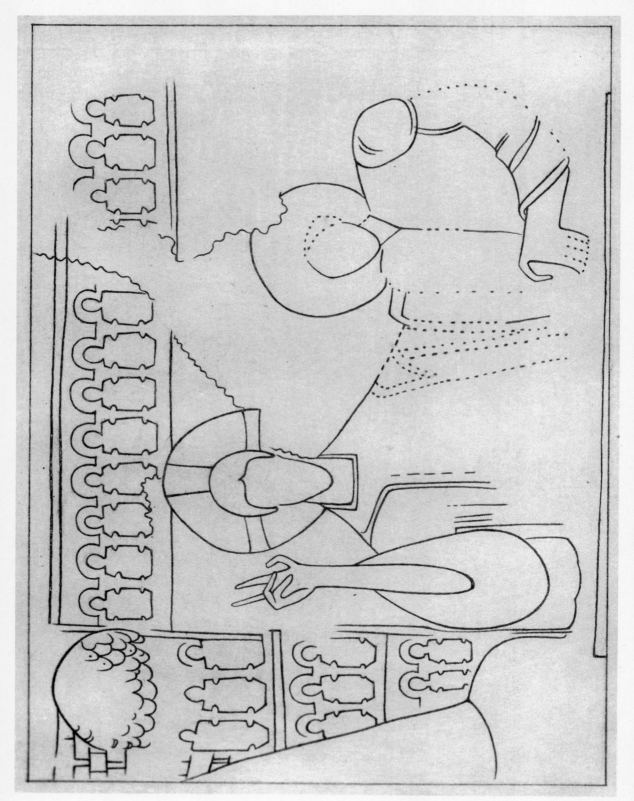

Plate 25   CHRIST DELIVERING THE BOOK TO ST. PAUL

Plate 26　DETAIL OF PLATE 25.

Plate 27   DETAIL OF PATTERN

HARDHAM

THESE paintings are more extensive in their range of subjects than the Clayton series, covering the walls of the chancel as well as the nave. Scenes from the Last Judgement are represented on the west wall and above the chancel arch in the nave as well as on the east, north and south walls of the chancel. The Fall is depicted on the west side of the chancel arch, while the lower tiers of the south and north walls of the nave are devoted to the story of Dives and Lazarus (?) and the life of St. George. On the upper tiers and the remainder of the east side of the chancel arch, extending into the lower tiers of the north and south walls of the chancel, there are scenes from the Life of Christ which seem to have included the last episodes of the Passion. Some of these are neatly divided by turrets and arches or set off on differently-patterned backgrounds.

The following belong to the Last Judgement cycle; four representations of the Torments of Hell on the west wall of the nave; opposite, over the chancel arch, two Censing Angels with what was probably the Agnus Dei in the centre; on the east wall of the chancel probably Christ in Majesty surrounded by Seraphim; a window inserted later has left only two of these figures. On both sides follow the Elders of the Apocalypse, each holding a vial and gittern; they continue on the upper tiers of the south and north walls of the chancel and were probably succeeded by Apostles and Prophets.

The Fall is represented as follows. On the left, above, is one of the best preserved pictures, showing Adam and Eve, who takes the fruit from the Serpent's mouth. Below, the Expulsion from the Garden was once depicted, but only the upper portion of the picture now remains, showing Adam and Eve with their hands raised in mourning. On the right side of the arch is a most original representation of Adam and Eve at work; the head of Adam appears above among trailing branches, perhaps pruning the vine. Below are the fragments of a figure of Eve, milking a large cow, which fills the centre of the picture.

The scenes from the life of Christ start in the nave on the right side of the chancel arch with the two well-preserved pictures of Annunciation and Visitation. The inscription above reads: Virgo salutatur, sterilis fecunda probatur. Continuing on the upper tier of the south wall of the nave is the Nativity with a group of shepherds (?), the appearance of the star (?), the three Magi on their journey (?), and last, possibly, Herod. On the upper tier of the north wall are the Adoration of the Magi, Joseph's Dream, and below, the Magi's Dream, the Flight into Egypt, the Fall of the Images (?), the Massacre of the Innocents, and perhaps the Presentation in the Temple. Returning to the chancel arch there follows on the left of the arch Christ among the Doctors. Of three scenes in the lower tier of the chancel arch only the Baptism of Christ remains. Traces of the last scenes from the Life of Christ can be found in the lower tiers of the south and north walls of the chancel, notably fragments of the Last Supper and the Three Marys at the Tomb.

In the lower tiers of the south wall of the nave is told the story of Dives and Lazarus. (?) The first scene from the Life of St. George on the north wall is claimed to be the Saint coming to the aid of the Christians at the battle of Antioch (1098), followed by his arrest and tortures.

Key - EAST AND WEST WALLS OF CHANCEL, HARDHAM, SHOWING POSITION OF PLATES 28 to 31.

Key - NORTH AND SOUTH WALLS, HARDHAM, SHOWING POSITION OF PLATES 32, 33, 34, 38, 39.

SCALE 0 1 2 3 4 5 6 7 8 9 10 FEET

Key - CHANCEL ARCH AND WEST WALL, HARDHAM, SHOWING POSITION OF PLATES 35, 36, 37, 40.

PLATES OF HARDHAM

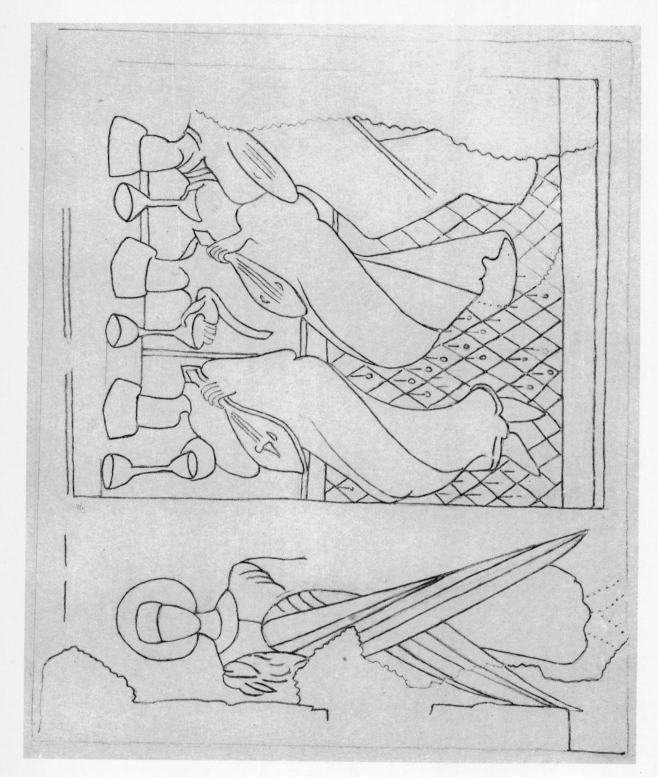

Plate 28   THREE ELDERS OF THE APOCALYPSE AND A SERAPH

Plate 30   THE EXPULSION FROM THE GARDEN OF EDEN

Plate 31   ADAM AND EVE AT WORK

Plate 32   VIRGIN AND CHILD, PART OF THE ADORATION OF THE MAGI

Plate 33   ST. GEORGE

Plate 34 MASSACRE OF THE INNOCENTS

Plate 35   CENSING ANGEL

Plate 36 THE ANNUNCIATION

Plate 37   THE BAPTISM OF CHRIST

Plate 38 NATIVITY

Plate 39   TWO OF THE MAGI ON THEIR JOURNEY

Plate 40   ONE SCENE OF THE TORMENTS OF HELL